# Dear Parents:

Congratulations! Your child is taking the first steps on an exciting journey. The destination? Independent reading!

**STEP INTO READING**® will help your child get there. The program offers five steps to reading success. Each step includes fun stories and colorful art or photographs. In addition to original fiction and books with favorite characters, there are Step into Reading Non-Fiction Readers, Phonics Readers and Boxed Sets, Sticker Readers, and Comic Readers—a complete literacy program with something to interest every child.

## Learning to Read, Step by Step!

### Ready to Read   Preschool–Kindergarten
• big type and easy words • rhyme and rhythm • picture clues
For children who know the alphabet and are eager to begin reading.

### Reading with Help   Preschool–Grade 1
• basic vocabulary • short sentences • simple stories
For children who recognize familiar words and sound out new words with help.

### Reading on Your Own   Grades 1–3
• engaging characters • easy-to-follow plots • popular topics
For children who are ready to read on their own.

### Reading Paragraphs   Grades 2–3
• challenging vocabulary • short paragraphs • exciting stories
For newly independent readers who read simple sentences with confidence.

### Ready for Chapters   Grades 2–4
• chapters • longer paragraphs • full-color art
For children who want to take the plunge into chapter books but still like colorful pictures.

**STEP INTO READING**® is designed to give every child a successful reading experience. The grade levels are only guides; children will progress through the steps at their own speed, developing confidence in their reading. The F&P Text Level on the back cover serves as another tool to help you choose the right book for your child.

Remember, a lifetime love of reading starts with a single step!

*For nurses everywhere—especially my favorite nurse,
Carla Murphy. There is no more important calling.
And in honor of the countless service workers with
the American Red Cross and my fellow volunteers
with the Travis Manion Foundation. —F.M.*

*To my grandparents Malcolm and Sylvia,
for helping me get where I needed to go —S.G.*

**Author acknowledgments:** *Many thanks for the expertise and fact-checking provided by Terry Reimer and, especially, Amelia Grabowski at the Clara Barton Missing Soldiers Office Museum in Washington, D.C. Much of the research that went into crafting this story was supported by the words of Clara Barton herself through the Clara Barton Papers at the Library of Congress and her book* The Story of My Childhood, *and by reading the biographies* Clara Barton: Professional Angel *by Elizabeth Brown Pryor and* The Life of Clara Barton *by Percy H. Epler. Many thanks for countless readings by the teachers and students at Holland Elementary and Afton Elementary, Andrea Mangold, and my family. Thank you to my incomparable editor and collaborator, Anna Membrino, for nursing this book along.*

**Editor acknowledgments:** *Special thanks to Susan Robbins Watson, Archivist and Manager of Historical Programs and Collections at the American Red Cross, for her assistance with this project.*

Visit us on the Web!
StepIntoReading.com
rhcbooks.com

Educators and librarians, for a variety of teaching tools, visit us at RHTeachersLibrarians.com

Library of Congress Cataloging-in-Publication Data is available upon request.
ISBN 978-1-5247-1557-1 (trade) — ISBN 978-1-5247-1558-8 (lib. bdg.) —
ISBN 978-1-5247-1559-5 (ebook)

Printed in the United States of America
10 9 8 7 6 5 4 3 2 1

This book has been officially leveled by using the F&P Text Level Gradient™ Leveling System.

# BRAVE CLARA BARTON

by Frank Murphy

illustrated by Sarah Green

Random House 🏠 New York

This is a story of a shy little girl
who grew to be brave.
Her name was Clara Barton.

Clara was born
on December 25, 1821,
in Massachusetts.
She was the baby
of the family.

Everyone taught her something!
Her father told her
epic stories of bravery
from the time he fought
in a war.

Her mother taught her
to know right from wrong.
Clara's sisters
were both teachers.
They taught her to read
by the age of three.

Clara was shy because
she had a lisp.
But her brother David
wanted her to take risks!

David put her on a horse
for the first time
before she was even
five years old.
David and Clara became
best friends!

When Clara was twelve,
her life changed.
David fell while
working in a barn.
His injuries were serious.
He couldn't walk.

Clara helped David
get stronger
and stronger.

Finally, two years later,
David could walk again!
Clara realized she liked
helping people.
But for those two years,
she barely went outside.
Her shyness grew worse.

Clara's parents wanted her
to overcome her shyness.
They told her to try teaching.
Clara was scared,
but she was also brave.

She taught summer school.

She loved helping her students.

Clara became more confident!

Clara moved to New Jersey
and started a one-room school.
She was a great teacher.
Soon Clara's little classroom
turned into a big school!

15

Clara was proud.

She wanted to become

the principal.

But a man was chosen instead.

People didn't think

a woman could lead a school.

Clara knew that was hogwash,

but she couldn't change

people's minds.

In 1861,
the United States
was having BIG trouble.

Many people in the North
believed that everyone
should live free.
Many people in the South
believed that it was their right
to own slaves.
The Southern states decided
to try to become
a separate country.

President Abraham Lincoln
was determined to keep
the country together
and to end slavery.
The Civil War started.
It was a war inside
the United States—
the North against the South.

Clara spent days and days
helping the wounded men.
She cooked meals for them.
She read to them.

But supplies were running out.

She wrote letters to her friends

in the North, asking them for help.

All of Clara's
letter writing paid off.
Soon she had enough
supplies to fill
three warehouses!
Clara left her job
to volunteer to help
the troops full-time.

The war continued.

Many soldiers needed help.

Clara knew if she were

on the battlefields

near the soldiers,

she could save more lives.

But one officer in the army
said women would
"skedaddle and create a panic."
Clara knew that was hogwash!

This time Clara wouldn't take "No!" for an answer! Soon the army organized some men to lead Clara to the battlefields. Clara shouted, "Follow the cannons!"

Clara knew

it would be dangerous.

Once,

she was kneeling,

helping an injured soldier.

She heard a bang.

A bullet flew

right through her sleeve!

It didn't even scratch Clara,

but it hit the soldier.

She couldn't save him.

He died in her arms.

All Clara could do
was turn to
the next injured soldier
and help him.

That is what Clara did
for the rest of the war.
She even helped
wounded soldiers
from the South.
Soon every soldier
knew her name.
But they called her
the Angel of the Battlefield.

In 1865, the war ended.
The North won.
Clara was happy
that slavery ended.
And she was happy
that the United States
stayed together.

But Clara found out
there were many
missing soldiers.
Families didn't know
what happened
to their relatives.
Clara asked President Lincoln
if she could help find them.
His answer was "YES!"

She received over 63,000 letters
from families asking for help.
And she answered each one!
She helped to discover
what happened to over
22,000 missing soldiers.

In 1869, Clara traveled to Europe.
There was a war there.
She joined a group called
the International Red Cross.
They helped soldiers in need.

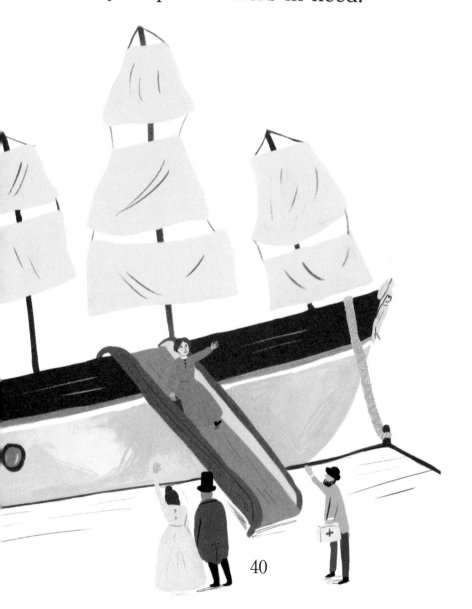

Kings and queens found out about
Clara's kindness.

They gave her
medals of honor
for helping their soldiers.

Clara came home
to the United States
with an idea!
She could help anyone in need!
So she started
the American Red Cross.

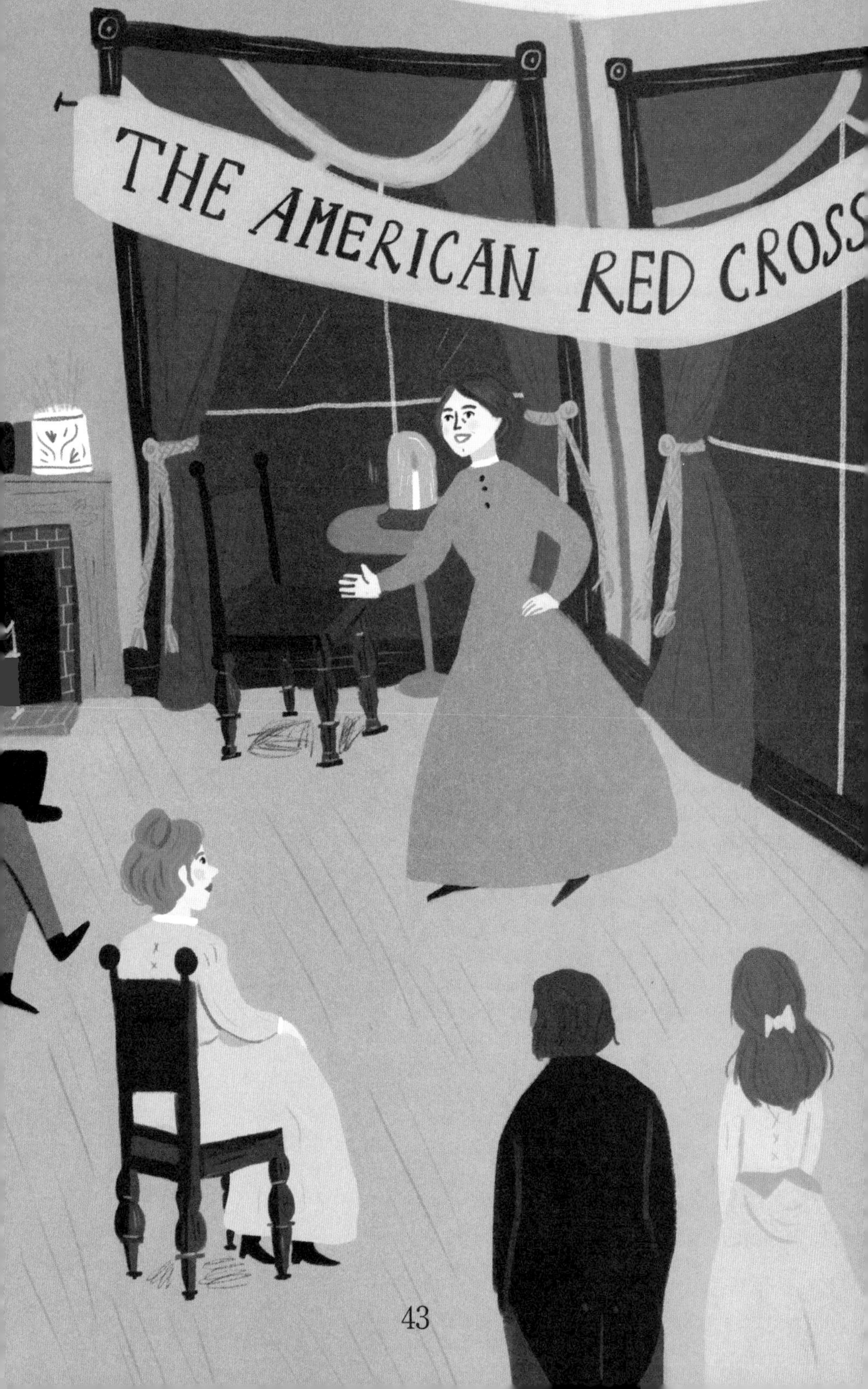
THE AMERICAN RED CROSS

When hurricanes hit,
Clara rushed to help.
When floods destroyed towns,
she and the Red Cross
came to their aid.

Clara kept helping people
until she was almost ninety!

Clara built up
the bravery inside her
and used it to help others.
She has inspired
generations of people
to serve humanity.

Can *you* find a way
to be brave
like Clara?

## Author's Note

Clara Barton was loved all around the world.
Once, she was honored by the king of Russia.
It was proper for people to curtsy or bow to
a king. When Clara began to curtsy, the king
stopped her! He bent over and helped raise her
back up. He told her, "Oh no, Miss Barton, not
you!" Even a king knew there was no one quite
like Clara.